NEBRASKA
HISTORY MOMENTS

STORIES & PHOTOS FROM THE
COLLECTIONS OF HISTORY NEBRASKA

David L. Bristow

History Nebraska · Lincoln

© 2021 History Nebraska
(Nebraska State Historical Society)
All rights reserved
history.nebraska.gov

ISBN: 978-0-933307-42-1
Library of Congress Control Number: 2021936192
Book design by Ben Kruse
Printed in the United States of America

30 29 28 27 26 25 24 23 22 21   2 3 4 5

Front cover: Circus performer Mildred Louise "Peggy" Johnson of Elsie, Nebraska, practices at the White Horse Ranch in 1953 (photo is reversed from original). Back cover: Fort Robinson, circa 1940. See pp. 68-69 for the stories behind these photos.

Frontispiece: Elvis fans, Omaha, 1956. See pp. 126-127. Reprinted with permission from The Omaha World-Herald.

CONTENTS

Foreword

Many history books focus on the big picture—how movements started, how laws were passed, and how communities were formed. There is merit in this, but the past is actually a mosaic. The larger image is made of many smaller pieces. This collection of 120 stories from Nebraska provides valuable insight into our shared past. Nebraska's history has stories of innovation and resilience, but also ones of challenges, hardship, and division. The study of history is complex and messy. But without an understanding of the past, how can we envision the future? Learning our history helps us imagine what our future might be.

Helping people use the past to create a better future is at the core of what History Nebraska does, and we are delighted to share this book with you. This collection of Nebraska History Moments originated as a series of daily emails shared with state senators and their staff while the Unicameral was in session. David Bristow has selected the most engaging examples to show some of the complexity and diversity of Nebraska's stories. I hope that these short pieces will make you laugh, think, and above all, be curious to learn more about Nebraska's rich history.

Trevor Jones
Director & CEO
History Nebraska

Preface

Most books are meant to be read straight through. Most writers of history start at the beginning and end at the end and hope that readers won't confuse things by skipping around.

This book is meant to be browsed. The stories don't follow a particular order. Read it back to front if you like. Open it at random and look at whatever catches your eye. Each page, each "moment," tells its own story. We will not be offended if this book finds a place on your nightstand, in your purse, on the floor of your truck, or in your bathroom.

If these history moments work as intended, you'll want to know more about them. Many of them are based on articles from *Nebraska History Magazine*, posts from our blog, or other online resources at our website, history.nebraska.gov. Go to history.nebraska.gov/books to find links for further reading and a place to sign up for a free, weekly Nebraska History Moments email featuring new stories not included here.

You can do all that and go no further. But we hope to draw you into our History Nebraska web, into a community of Nebraskans who are insatiably curious about the past that lies under our feet and all around us. We hope you'll follow us on social media, visit our museum and historic sites, read *Nebraska History Magazine*, and support our work through your membership.

What is our work? With a few exceptions, the photos and artifacts in these pages come from the collections of History Nebraska (aka the Nebraska State Historical Society). We have been collecting and interpreting the state's past since 1878, and during that time we have curated the largest and best collection in existence of Nebraska photos, archives, and artifacts. We do this in order to tell meaningful stories that connect the past with the present.

That is a huge task, and it means that while this little book may be the work of one author, it is built on the cumulative efforts of colleagues past and present. Much of what I tell you about these photos and objects comes from metadata and finding aids prepared by our curators. Our collections team includes librarian Cindy Drake, audio/visual curator Paul Eisloeffel, anthropology curator Nic Fogerty, digital archivist Lindsey Hillgartner, photo curator Karen Keehr, government records curator Gayla Koerting, museum registrar Jordan Miller, museum curator Laura Mooney, and manuscripts curator Tom Mooney. They and their predecessors—going back a nearly a century and a half—built these collections. Most of these photos were digitally scanned by Dale Bacon, Dell Darling, Jill Koelling, Mary-Jo Miller, Marty Miller, Curt Peacock, Joel Thoreson, and many dedicated volunteers. Mary Woltemath spent years microfilming Nebraska newspapers.

I'm indebted to other colleagues who have since retired—Pat Gaster—or passed on: historians Jim Potter, John Carter, Tom Buecker, and archeologist Gale Carlson. Relevant links to their writing and to that of other Nebraska historians can be found at history.nebraska.gov/books. My thanks also to John Strope for proofreading and suggestions. Any errors that remain are my responsibility alone.

Nebraska History Moments will show you many surprising things about Nebraska's past. It will touch on some of history's larger themes, but it won't show you the big picture in a continuous narrative. For that, we recommend another small book published by History Nebraska: Ron Naugle's *A Brief History of Nebraska*.

It takes only a moment to discover something new about our past. I hope you enjoy reading these *Nebraska History Moments* as much as I've enjoyed writing them.

DLB

Footrace in Bartlett

Wheeler County, circa 1913

Photographer John Nelson captured the moment the runner crossed the scratched-in-the-dirt finish line.

Look closer. This is no formal athletic event. The competitors are dressed up in nice clothes and are running in stocking feet. It's a special occasion of some kind, but the race itself is just for fun.

And not everyone is interested. The boy at left is watching the photographer instead.

John Nelson was born in Sweden in 1864 and came to Nebraska with his parents when he was seventeen. He opened a photography studio in Ericson around 1900. Today History Nebraska has his photos. Pictures he made of his neighbors now tell stories of a vanished time.

The same is true of countless artifacts, documents, and other records at History Nebraska. If you look closely, moments from the past tell little stories, and together they tell big stories.

That is what this book is about.

Pawnee Women and Girls

Nance County, undated

People have been living in Nebraska for at least 13,000 years. We have to rely on archeological evidence for all but the past few centuries.

The Pawnees are the earliest of the historic Native tribes to live in what we now call Nebraska. (By "historic" we mean the period for which we have written records.) The Pawnees were here at least by the sixteenth century, but they may have arrived as early as the twelfth.

The Pawnees lived in earth lodge villages. They were farmers, planting corn, beans, squash, and sunflowers. They also hunted bison part of the year. Numbering 15,000 to 20,000 people when Europeans arrived on the Great Plains, the tribe was soon ravaged by imported diseases, leaving only about 2,000 people by the 1870s.

In 1873 the tribe was hunting bison in southwestern Nebraska when they were ambushed by the Lakotas at a site now known as Massacre Canyon. This and other hardships led to Pawnees to agree, reluctantly, to US government plans to remove them to Indian Territory (Oklahoma) in 1875.

Šebesta Family Trunk

Saline and Fillmore counties, circa 1910

Imagine what it would be like to leave your country behind, taking with you only what would fit inside a wooden box.

Ignac and Marie Šebesta did just that when they immigrated to the United States around 1910, two of many Czech immigrants bound for Nebraska. They packed this trunk—now in the collections of the Nebraska History Museum—and carefully painted their name and destination on the lid (though Tobias is actually in Saline County).

The Šebestas started out as farm laborers in Milligan and Tobias. They were better off than some: many immigrants could not afford a trunk and packed their belongings in cloth bags.

What was once an ordinary trunk now represents a history held in common by many Nebraska families.

Almost the Capital City
Bellevue, 1856 drawing

Were it not for Francis Burt's digestive problems, Bellevue might be Nebraska's big city and Omaha its suburb. History is full of odd contingencies.

This sketch shows Bellevue in 1856, two years after the town missed its chance to become our capital city.

Francis Burt was Nebraska Territory's first governor. A presidential appointee, he arrived in Bellevue on October 7, 1854. Why Bellevue? Towns were springing up all along the west bank of the Missouri River, but Bellevue was more established, having served as a trading post and Indian mission for decades. Burt apparently intended to convene the legislature there.

But the governor had fallen seriously ill during the four-week journey from his native South Carolina. He died on October 18. During the next crucial months, territorial secretary Thomas Cuming served as acting governor. Cuming was allied with the founders of Omaha City and made it the capital, a status it maintained until after statehood.

Nebraska's First Capitol
Omaha, 1855

This was Nebraska Territory's first capitol. It was also Omaha's first brick building, built by the Council Bluffs and Nebraska Ferry Company with Iowa bricks. It stood on Ninth Street between Farnam and Douglas.

"The building is a neat and substantial one, but altogether too small for the purpose intended," said the *Nebraska Palladium* (Bellevue) on January 17, 1855, the day after the first legislature convened. The front door opened into a hallway, with the House of Representatives chamber on the left and the governors' apartment on the right. A winding staircase led upstairs to the Council chamber (equivalent to a Senate) and committee rooms.

In 1858 the legislature moved to a larger building on the present site of Central High School. The old capitol was later razed, but it had served its purpose. It helped establish Omaha as Nebraska Territory's capital city.

David City Base Ball Club

1894

"Champion Amateur Team of Nebraska," proclaims the label on this photo. The later term "semi-pro" would be a better description. Before radio or TV, "base ball" (as it was spelled at the time) was so popular that small town teams commonly brought in players from larger cities. Reporting on a game that August, the *Omaha Bee* noted that David City had "three colored men from Kansas City," while opposing Schuyler was "braced up" with a few (White) players from Omaha.

But this isn't a story of progress toward racial integration. Post-Reconstruction-era America was moving backward, becoming more segregated. In professional baseball, a few Black players played in the major leagues in the 1880s, with a larger number in the minor leagues. The unofficial "color line" was established through all levels of baseball by 1900.

Railroad Water Tower

Perkins County, circa 1900

Steam locomotives required coaling stations along their route. They also needed to take on water for their boilers every ten miles or so. A railroad worker would jerk a rope attached to the drop-down nozzle shown here and release it when the boiler was filled.

A steam engine's frequent need for water is why Nebraska's many railroad towns are spaced as they are. Many Nebraska towns got their start as water-and-coal stations along the way. And because of these towers they became known as "jerkwater towns."

Had Nebraska been settled before the railroad era, the location and layout of many of our communities would be different.

Mystery Grave

Boyd County, 2012

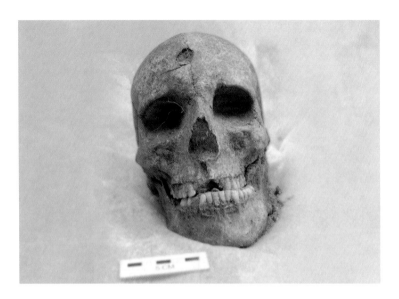

Like something out of detective fiction, a crew digging a trench found an unmarked grave in a rural field far from known cemeteries. The skull had what looked like a bullet hole in the forehead.

Local authorities contacted the State Archeology Office at History Nebraska. Was this a crime scene? Archeologists excavated. Based on the bones, they concluded that this was a man in his twenties or thirties. Based on coffin hardware, the burial took place between the 1880s and 1910.

The body has since been reburied in a Boyd County cemetery. But who was it? Further research led to the story of Jack Richards, said to be the accomplice of two cattle thieves who were lynched in Holt County in 1894.

The following year Richards was driving a wagon through Boyd County when he stopped to rest his team. He entered a cornfield to pick some ears for his horses, but the landowner came after him with a slug-loaded shotgun. A gunfight ensued and Richards was shot in the forehead, dying two days later. The farmer was acquitted of murder charges.

Nebraska's First Unicameral Session

Lincoln, January 5, 1937

US Senator George Norris of McCook was the best-known supporter of a unicameral legislature. A one-house legislature eliminated the conference committees that Norris believed were ripe for abuse. The ruling party often used the House-Senate conference committee to rewrite legislation to favor its own positions.

Norris also believed that the legislature should be nonpartisan. He wanted to make it more difficult for party leaders to control individual senators, and wanted to make it easier for individual Republicans and Democrats to cooperate on bills of mutual interest.

Opponents argued that a small legislature would be prone to "roller coaster lawmaking," but many Nebraskans liked the idea of having fewer salaries to pay with their tax dollars. Nebraskans voted to adopt the unicameral system in 1934, the first and only state to do so.

Lakota Family at Train Depot
Alliance, 1930s

A labor shortage during World War I left western Nebraska potato farmers facing the loss of their crops. They brought in Lakota (Sioux) Indians as harvesters, beginning an annual tradition that lasted from 1917 through the 1950s. Here, at the Burlington depot in Alliance, a Lakota family poses for a photo wearing some items that were probably used in the annual Lakota post-harvest dance in the city.

The choice of costume sends a message. The reservation era brought tremendous pressure for Native peoples to abandon their cultural identities. The Lakotas themselves had different ideas. This family presents themselves to the photographer simultaneously as modern and "respectable" in the eyes of White people, and yet unapologetically Native.

Unloading Sugar Beets
Morrill, Scotts Bluff County, 1920s

Detail of above photo.

At first glance this looks like the strangest railroad bridge ever—up and back down in an impossibly tight curve. But look at the detail above. It's a wagon ramp between the tracks. Farmers pitched their sugar beets into a railcar below.

Introduced locally as early as 1901, the sugar beet proved well suited to the North Platte Valley's soil and climate. Irrigated acreage expanded greatly after the North Platte Project began delivering water in 1909. The area's first beet processing facility opened in 1910. Two decades later, Great Western Sugar's six plants across the valley were producing 250 million pounds of sugar per year.

A Cotton Mill in Nebraska?

Kearney, circa 1893

Nebraska isn't known for textile mills, but we had one briefly in the 1890s. The two-story mill opened in the spring of 1892, employing hundreds of workers—many of them women and children. Each year they transformed some 50,000 bales of Texas cotton into 76,000 yards of fabric.

Success was short-lived. Drought and depression in 1893, coupled with increased freight charges, stressed the company. In winter the water-powered mill periodically ground to a halt when the canal froze. Unanticipated fuel costs helped force the mill into bankruptcy in 1901.

Clara Bewick Colby & The Woman's Tribune

Beatrice

Nebraska ratified the Nineteenth Amendment in August 1919. But Nebraska women were deeply involved in the campaign for voting rights long before that.

The Woman's Tribune (1883-1909) was one of the nation's most important and longest-running suffrage newspapers—and it was published in Beatrice, Nebraska. Publisher Clara Bewick Colby (right) is shown in 1890 with sculptor Bessie Potter Vonnoh and Susan B. Anthony (seated).

The *Tribune* began as the official paper of the Nebraska Woman Suffrage Association, and in 1886-89 was the official paper of the National Woman Suffrage Association. Available at History Nebraska, it remains an important resource for historians, as Colby printed a lot of news and documents not preserved elsewhere.

El Ramon Londres Cigar Box

Grand Island, early 1900s

Where were El Ramon Londres cigars made? Cuba, perhaps? How about Grand Island, Nebraska?

The tobacco, of course, was grown farther south, but by the early twentieth century Nebraska had more than 200 cigar manufacturers, producing nearly 30 million cigars a year.

Many of these "factories" were cottage industries located in a home or perhaps an adjoining shed. Two or three people made cigars by hand, using wooden molds. But some were big operations. In 1916 Hastings had six cigar factories producing seven million cigars per year. Cigars declined in popularity with the growth of cigarette smoking during and after World War I.

KOIL Radio Sound Effects
Omaha, August 24, 1937

   Radio became a source of news and entertainment starting in the 1920s. National networks emerged by the end of that decade, but local programming rounded out the broadcast day.

   With nothing to see, radio dramas and comedies required listeners to use their imaginations. Listeners constructed the visuals in their own heads based only on narration, dialogue, and the perfect timing of the sound-effects man.

Then and Now: O Street Floodwaters
Lincoln, 1908

History Nebraska sometimes blends old and new photos of the same location. It's a fun way to bring the past into the present for our social media followers. Here, two young men brave the floodwaters just east of 12th on O Street. They're hamming it up for the photographer; there is no way that motorcycle is still running.

Major flooding in 1950 and 1951 led to the construction of ten dams in the Salt Creek watershed by the US Army Corps of Engineers, and thirty smaller upstream dams by the Soil Conservation Service (now the Natural Resources Conservation Service). Lincoln has not had a major flood since those projects were completed.

Chrisman Sisters, Homesteaders

Custer County, 1886

Photographer Solomon D. Butcher wrote that a rancher's "four daughters took advantage of the homestead, timber claim, and pre-emption laws, each holding three claims and having shacks similar to this one on their claims, there two or more girls taking turns about living with the other in order to comply with the law." Many unmarried women and widows claimed homesteads.

To claim land, you had to build a house and live there for a certain period before receiving a deed. This was meant to discourage speculators and reward genuine settlers. While many people sold their land as soon as they "proved up," only a small percentage of claims were fraudulent.

All this took place on land that had until recently belonged to Native peoples. The federal government removed people from various parts of Nebraska before large-scale homesteading began. Few Nebraska homesteaders saw their predecessors.

Those Fish Stories

Verdigre, Neligh, and Valentine, 1907

Exaggeration postcards were popular in the early twentieth century. Photos of animals, pumpkins, or ears of corn were carefully blown up in the darkroom and pasted onto other photos as a humorous promotion of Nebraska's bounty.

This photo refers to an even older tradition: the fish tale. In 1907 the *Norfolk Daily News* reported that newspapers in Verdigre, Neligh, and Valentine were apparently trying to top each other, with the tales growing as they moved west.

Verdigre told of a local man catching a three-pounder that was then swallowed by a large catfish. Neligh then reported a similar story, with the second fish swallowed by an even bigger fish. Valentine topped them all by reporting how local people came to the rescue of what they thought was a drowning person that turned out to be a 102-pound catfish.

"The further west you go the more progressive the people," the Norfolk editor observed.

Broken Bow's Three Rival Newspapers

Custer County, 1886-88

Even small towns often had rival newspapers in the late nineteenth century. We can see Broken Bow's early newspaper buildings thanks to Solomon Butcher, whose 3,500 glass plate negatives are preserved in the collections of History Nebraska.

Broken Bow was platted in 1882. The first train arrived in 1886, by which time the *Omaha Daily Bee* credited the town with a thousand residents, eight general stores, four drug stores, three hardware stores, three hotels, and three well-edited newspapers.

Shown here are the offices of the *Republican* (in a soddie!), the *Nebraska Statesman* (a "red hot Democratic paper"), and the *Custer Leader*, another Republican paper, judging by the 1888 Benjamin Harrison campaign poster in its front window.

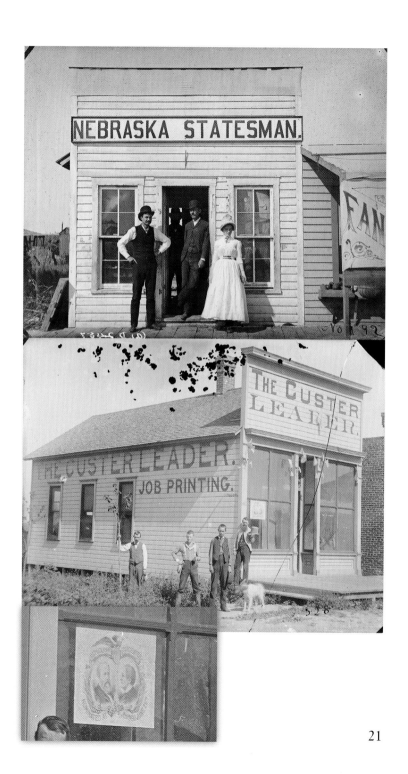

Neligh Mill

Neligh, circa 1885

John D. Neligh used locally fired brick to build a mill in 1873. It was the first business in the town named in his honor. A good mill helped many Nebraska towns grow in the 1870s-80s. Mills ground local grain into flour, cutting costs for long-distance shipping.

Neligh Mill was powered by the Elkhorn River. Here you can see the mill dam and penstock (which looks like a big wooden box beside the river). The penstock held the water turbine, which was connected to the building by a drive cable (and later, a big leather belt).

Neligh had an ample water supply and was on a main rail line, allowing it to fill lucrative contracts for the US Army and the Bureau of Indian Affairs, and to sell flour for overseas export.

Neligh Mill Flour Sack

Neligh, circa 1900-1915

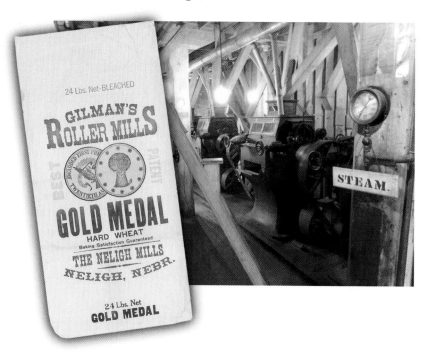

Do you buy flour by the 24-pound sack? You would if you baked all your family's bread.

Gold Medal flour was produced at Neligh Mill and packed in cloth bags made by Omaha's Bemis Bag Company. General Mills bought the Gold Medal trademark in 1940 to eliminate confusion with their similarly-named flour.

S. F. Gilman owned Neligh Mill from 1894 until his death in 1915. That year the mill changed its power source from the Elkhorn River to a diesel engine.

Today Neligh Mill State Historic Site is operated by History Nebraska. Most of the old milling equipment is still in place.

Crazy Horse's Grave

Sheridan County, October 1877

People have tried for years to determine where the legendary Lakota war leader is buried. Yet here is this photograph taken on a hilltop overlooking Camp Sheridan near Hay Springs, Nebraska. Historians accept its identification as "Crazy Horse's Grave."

But this wasn't a permanent grave. This was a burial scaffold in the Lakota tradition. After Crazy Horse was killed at Fort Robinson, his parents brought his body to Beaver Creek, where they lived, and scaffolded it for two months. A fence was added because of grazing cattle. Later the family permanently buried Crazy Horse's bones elsewhere—and it is that location that remains secret.

A Mugshot Headlock

Omaha Police Court, 1899

Herbert Cockran had to be restrained for his 1899 Omaha Police Court mug shot. Photography revolutionized crime investigations. Starting in 1867, the State Penitentiary used photography to identify its prisoners. The Omaha Police Court later photographed suspects on arrest and recorded physical characteristics for future identification. Starting in the early 1900s, the US military and some police departments began recording fingerprints as a unique identifier.

Cornhusker Ordnance Plant

Grand Island, 1940s

These women are packing explosives into bomb casings. During World War II, women did tough—and sometimes dangerous—jobs traditionally seen as men's work.

Built in 1942, the Cornhusker Ordnance Plant sprawled across a twenty-square-mile area west of Grand Island. Nebraska was home to several large wartime plants. At one point during the war, the Naval Ammunition Depot in Hastings was making more than 40 percent of the US Navy's munitions. The Sioux Army Depot near Sidney stored massive quantities of ammunition and other materiel. The Martin Bomber Plant in Bellevue built B-26 and B-29 bombers. Other towns had air bases or prisoner of war camps. New workers flocking to these towns boosted local economies and created housing shortages.

Train Wreck

Indianola, 1911

A head-on collision of two passenger trains near Indianola killed eighteen people and injured many more on May 29, 1911. The *McCook Republican* called the wreck "the worst ever known on this division of the Burlington Railroad and possibly west of the Missouri River."

Railroad fatalities grew as trains became bigger, faster, and carried more passengers. During the peak year nationally for railroad accidents, 1907, trains were the largest single cause of violent death, and had a fatality rate 110 times greater than that of modern airlines.

Controlling the Trains

McCook, 1947

This machine was designed to prevent collisions like the one shown on the previous page. In 1947 this was the peak of railroad technology.

It's called Centralized Traffic Control, a form of railroad signaling in which switches and stop-and-proceed signals are controlled from a central office. This replaced the older system of routing trains by local signal operators or by the train crews themselves. A dispatcher was constantly aware of the position of each train as it was electrically reported along the route. It was the predecessor of today's computerized systems.

This CTC machine was moved from Brush, Colorado. In McCook it controlled a subdivision of the Chicago, Burlington & Quincy Railroad between Akron and Derby, Colorado. Two similar machines in McCook controlled the Burlington tracks between McCook and Akron and between McCook and Hastings.

The CTC machine went in through an upper-story window. You can almost hear the men complaining, "Why can't we put it on the ground floor?"

Frederick Douglass's Nebraska Sister

Omaha, 1893-94

Frederick Douglass is remembered for his escape from slavery and for his work on behalf of freedom and civil rights. A series of letters uncovered in Lincoln reveal that Douglass came to Omaha in 1893 to look for his sister, Ruth Cox Adams.

Douglass and Adams weren't biological siblings, but at one time they thought they were. The sale of enslaved people to different owners often split up families and obscured family relationships. Douglass, who was separated from his mother at an early age, called family separation one of slavery's worst cruelties.

When Fred and Ruth learned they weren't blood relatives, they continued to think of themselves as adopted siblings. Eventually they lost touch after they each moved to different parts of the country. Fred heard that Ruth was living in Omaha, but she had moved by the time he arrived. A few years later he learned she was living in Norfolk, Nebraska, and they resumed their correspondence.

History Nebraska owns a sewing box (shown above) that Douglass gave to Adams, and a lock of Douglass's hair.

Dust Storm

Alma, Harlan County, April 7, 1935

The Dust Bowl in "the Dirty Thirties" was one of the America's worst environmental disasters. Deep plowing of semi-arid grassland, followed by severe drought, produced millions of barren acres ready to blow away. Half a million people lost their homes; many left the Great Plains for good. Oklahoma and Texas saw the worst of it, but southwestern Nebraska counties suffered, too.

Alma is located along the Republican River in south central Nebraska. A month and a half after this dust storm, a severe flash flood swept down the river valley through several counties, destroying homes and farms and killing more than 100 people.

Hammer Gang

Lincoln, circa 1915

How long would it take you to drive a five-foot tent stake into the ground with a seventeen-pound hammer? Not long at all if you work as a team.

When the circus hit town, the roustabouts, canvas crews, and hammer gangs had little time to get the tents and rigging ready for the first matinee. *McClure's Magazine* reported in 1895 that it took 200 to 300 blows to drive a five-foot tent stake. Standing in a circle, the hammer gang swung their hammers with such precision that a stake received seven blows per second. A good crew could sink a thousand stakes in forty-five minutes.

Bellevue Ferry

June 14, 1924

Ferries have been crossing the Missouri River since the territorial days, but this one is from the automobile era. For years there was no convenient way for southwestern Iowa farmers to reach the South Omaha stockyards with truckloads of livestock. The Douglas Street Bridge was the nearest crossing.

Despite demand, ferry businesses struggled to survive in Bellevue. Blame the ever-shifting channel and banks of the Missouri River. A well-prepared landing could be rendered unapproachable by shifting sandbars, and building a new landing also meant building a new road.

The completion of the South Omaha Bridge in 1936 rendered the Bellevue ferry obsolete.

Cottonwood Springs

Lincoln County, 1860s

In the early days of the Oregon, California, and Mormon trails, travelers had to pack everything they needed before they left the Missouri River. There were no towns or stores along the trail, though many people traded with Native Americans on the way.

By 1850 the army built a few forts along the route, such as Fort Kearny. Later, entrepreneurs opened "road ranches" that offered food and supplies, animals for trade, a post office, and maybe a blacksmith.

The Cottonwood Springs road ranche stood near present-day North Platte. It also served as a Pony Express station in 1860-61. After the Dakota War of 1862, the army built Fort McPherson nearby.

Road Ranche

Kimball County, 1876

Here's another road ranche. This is the 1870s version of an I-80 truck stop.

By 1876 the railroads had siphoned off a lot of overland traffic, but other travelers still relied on road ranches to provide food, supplies, wagon repair, and fresh horses to trade. This one was owned by Tom Evans near Antelopeville, a settlement that in 1885 changed its name to Kimball.

The white picket fence adds a homey touch. This was not only a place of business, but also a home.

Eve of Game Day

Lincoln, 1930

This photo was taken the night before a key Big Six football matchup between Missouri and Nebraska. On November 14, 1930, Cornhusker fans gathered for a pre-game rally at the Hotel Lincoln, 143 N. 9th Street.

Why would home team fans rally at a hotel? For the enlightenment of traveling Missourians, perhaps?

More likely the hotel was full of Nebraskans in town to watch the game. In an era of slower travel, an overnight stay in Lincoln would have been necessary for more in-state fans than today.

The game ended in a 0-0 tie, an even lower-scoring contest than the previous year's 7-7 tie in Columbia, Missouri.

Lillie's Cornhusker

Rockford, Gage County, 1890s

This is what it really means to be a Cornhusker: picking corn by hand after the first frost, shucking it, and throwing into the wagon. Imagine doing a whole field that way.

Farmers used to shuck corn with a husking peg. This was a round piece of hardwood, sharpened on one end and held in place with a loop of buckskin. In the early 1890s William Lillie of Rockford invented the hook-and-glove device shown here.

"He succeeded in every way except financially," a historian wrote. The Lillie cornhusker was used in Nebraska as late as the 1920s. Similar devices were in use for another few decades. Gradually, more and more farms began using mechanical pickers.

The photos show Lillie posing with his invention, plus a Lillie cornhusker from History Nebraska's collection.

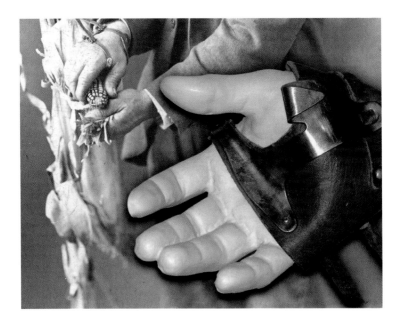

Union Stockyards

Omaha, 1949

South Omaha was a meatpacking town from the start. It was founded in 1883 on a site chosen for easy access to rail and river transportation. It grew so fast that people called it the "Magic City." Within a decade it was the nation's third-largest meat-packing center. The work drew immigrant labor, and then as now the city was ethnically diverse.

Omaha annexed South Omaha in 1915. Forty years later Omaha surpassed Chicago as the world's largest meatpacking center. Technological changes decentralized meatpacking in the following decades, and the once-mighty Union Stockyards closed in 1999.

Mailbags in the Snow

Marquette, Hamilton County, early 1900s

We don't know the story behind this postcard photo. Marquette never had much more than 300 people at its peak in 1930. Are these mailbags all for local delivery? Or might they have been pulled from a snowbound Burlington train?

The US Post Office boasted that it was stopped by "neither snow nor rain nor heat nor gloom of night." South of Marquette in Aurora, Wayne Arthur Shaneyfelt worked as a mail carrier from the 1930s into the 1970s. When he started, carriers on city routes walked their entire routes twice a day—about 12 to 15 miles in all.

Writing for *I Remember… Family Stories from Hamilton County, Nebraska* (1999), Shaneyfelt recalled his "roughest day" during his first winter. Aurora didn't require people to scoop their sidewalks, and every house had a front-porch mailbox. That morning he waded through two-foot-deep snow—and did it again that afternoon. Everyone received their mail.

Ken Eddy's Drive-In

48th and "O" Streets, Lincoln, July 11, 1952

Why go inside the restaurant when you can eat in your car? There's nothing like the sticky texture of spilled pop on vinyl upholstery (cars didn't have cupholders), or the wonder of discovering a months-old French fry under the driver's seat.

Why did anyone think this was a good idea?

But they did. Drive-ins weren't new in the 1950s, but became icons of mid-century automobile culture. Nebraska's home-grown drive-ins lured motorists with bold signage, from the UFO-inspired Scotty's Drive-In in Scottsbluff, to the neon cowboy above Bronco's Hamburgers in Omaha. Ken Eddy's sign featured a three-color starburst.

Bert Martin

Keya Paha County, 1900

Bert Martin was a ranch hand in Keya Paha County. In 1900 he was sent to the State Penitentiary for two years for stealing a horse. A weeping woman stood by his side at the sentencing. A baby in her arms, she was said to be Bert's wife.

Eleven months later, Martin's cellmate told authorities that Martin was a woman. "She is distinctly masculine in appearance," the *Lincoln Evening News* reported on October 12, 1901. Bert's legal name was Lena Martin, but many of his friends in Keya Paha County refused to believe the news.

Words such as transgender, intersex, and non-binary were not yet in use. Instead, Gov. Ezra P. Savage used dehumanizing language, calling Martin "a sexual monstrosity, unfit for association with men or women even in a penal institution." Savage commuted Martin's sentence "on the solemn promise of its aged mother to care for it and guard it."

Omaha Nation Effigy Bowl

Present-day Thurston County, late 1700s-early 1800s

This wooden bowl at the Nebraska History Museum is thought to be one of the oldest examples of Plains woodcarving held in a museum collection. It dates from the late eighteenth or early nineteenth century. It is a rare enough object that in recent years it has been loaned for exhibitions in Paris and New York City.

But why the unusual shape? Turn it over and it looks like a swimming beaver, gliding half submerged across a river's surface.

Western Nebraska's "Ghost Counties"
1867-1877

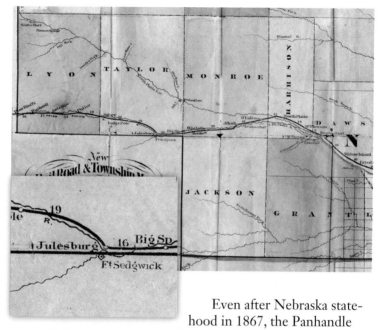

Even after Nebraska statehood in 1867, the Panhandle was so little known to mapmakers that six fake counties appeared on maps for ten years.

The Colton mapmaking company of New York published an 1867 map showing the Panhandle counties of Lyon, Taylor, Monroe, Harrison, Jackson, and Grant. Together they covered almost one-fifth of the state, but none existed. Other mapmakers copied them and they appeared on maps as late as 1877.

How did this happen? Brian Croft of Scottsbluff found the answer in History Nebraska's government records collection. He discovered a legislative bill to create the six counties. Colton put it on the map, but the bill never became law.

Courtesy of Colin and Brian Croft, these 1870 map details also show Julesburg in Nebraska instead of Colorado—which even fooled US Census workers!

The "Saloonn" in Scottsbluff

circa 1900

Scottsbluff started with a dirt main street and a misspelled "SALOONN." Founded in 1899-1900, Scottsbluff was the not the first town along the North Platte River. Gering residents will have you know that their city has occupied the south side of the river since 1887.

But even Gering was founded two decades after the first western Nebraska towns sprang up along the Union Pacific Railroad, and more than three decades after eastern Nebraska's Missouri River towns were founded in the 1850s. Two new developments fueled the rapid growth of Scottsbluff in the early twentieth century: large-scale irrigation and the sugar beet industry.

Little Girl on the Ledge at Central Hospital
Lincoln, 1915

Is that a little girl on the ledge, or a large and realistic-looking doll?

Central Hospital was located at 2116-2120 O Street, where there is now a bridge across Antelope Creek. It was one of nearly a dozen mostly small, private hospitals and sanitariums profiled in "Lincoln a Health Resort of Prominence" in the local *Will Maupin's Weekly* on April 26, 1912. Central's "spacious sun porches, shaded walks, and other attractions appeal to the eye and the tired brain, and contribute to the personal ease and comfort so necessary in sickness."

The hospital was staffed by "leading physicians and surgeons" and boasted "one of the largest X-ray machines in the west." Which might come in handy if your child somehow fell off a house and broke something.

Looking East along Farnam Street

Omaha, 1889

No longer a frontier town, Omaha boasted substantial brick buildings, pavement, streetcars, and telephone and electrical wires. "I guess there ain't any end to Omaha," 16-year-old Frisby Rasp of Gresham, Nebraska, wrote to his parents in 1888. "You can walk till you are tired out in any direction you choose, and the houses are as thick as ever…. It is dusty just as soon as it quits raining, and the dust here is the worst dust I ever saw. It is all stone and manure. Streets that ain't paved, 2 feet deep of mud."

Depression-Era Relief Office

Hastings, 1934

RELIEF OFFICE · HASTINGS · ADAMS CO.
1-6-23

To a modern eye, these unemployed people seem overdressed to sign up for relief benefits. In a more formal time, people still dressed up to go shopping downtown. But this also looks like an effort to maintain dignity through the Great Depression and show that they were not "the poor."

Hastings, like other Nebraska communities, benefitted from New Deal programs that created jobs for unemployed workers. But these jobs were often temporary and paid minimal wages. US entry into World War II provided a bigger economic boost. As home to the Naval Ammunition Depot, by 1942 Hastings had so many jobs paying good wages that the city became a magnet for workers, creating a severe local housing shortage during the war years.

Cudahy Packing Co.

South Omaha, circa 1906

Cudahy was one of the "Big Four" meatpackers in early South Omaha, the "Magic City" that sprang up around the Union Stockyards starting in 1884. Their plant was at 33rd and N streets.

This publicity photo tells a story of Progressive Era politics. In 1904, Upton Sinclair's novel *The Jungle* shocked readers with its graphic portrayal of the meatpacking industry's filthy and dangerous conditions. This, plus exposés by muckraking journalists, led in 1906 to the federal Pure Food and Drug Act and the Meat Inspection Act.

Cudahy reassures the public in the photo's caption: "The Bureau inspector assigned to sausage department supervises the entire process of manufacturing. His duties are to know that only clean, sweet and wholesome meats are used, prevent the use of prohibited preservatives and adulterations and look after the sanitation of the department."

Groundbreaking, Nebraska State Capitol
Lincoln, April 15, 1922

Today's Nebraska State Capitol is the third capitol built on the same spot in Lincoln. The first two were traditional in design and poorly constructed. The third was boldly modern in design. It was the first "skyscraper" commissioned for a state capitol, and designed in the trendy "art deco" style. The state government spent ten years building the capitol on a pay-as-you-go plan. It came in under budget.

Here we see the formal groundbreaking ceremony. Governor Samuel McKelvie would have disdained the golden shovels and pre-dug dirt of modern groundbreakings. The press noted with approval that the governor—the former editor of the *Nebraska Farmer*—plowed a good, straight furrow.

University of Nebraska

Founded in 1869, shown in 1872

The University of Nebraska was founded on high ideals in 1869. The original charter called for free tuition, banned discrimination based on "age, sex, color, or nationality," and said the institution would serve the state's "inhabitants" and not just its citizens. Nebraska boosters hoped to build the state's population with immigration.

A modern university was still a new idea, and not all Nebraskans felt it was necessary. Even the agricultural campus was criticized as impractical "book farming."

What was it like to be a student? If you like leaky roofs, chilly classrooms, and traditional memorize-and-recite schooling, you'd love 1870s NU classes. It took twenty years for the university to develop into a modern institution with professional faculty, lectures, and research-based learning.

Shown here, University Hall stood at the north end of 11th Street. It was razed in 1948, but a state historical marker marks the spot on campus.

WWII "Short Snorter"

Doniphan, 1945

A short snorter is paper money signed by people traveling together or meeting up at different events. The tradition started among Alaskan bush pilots in the 1920s, and peaked in popularity during World War II. If a signer asked you to produce your short snorter and didn't have it, you owed them a drink. ("Short snort" was slang for a less-than-full shot of liquor.)

Loyde H. Adams was born in Doniphan in 1919. He created this elaborate short snorter while serving in the Army Air Force in the southwest Pacific. By war's end it had grown to 62 banknotes taped together, including Japanese military currency and invasion money from the Philippines and the Netherlands, plus Chinese, Australian, Indian, and American bills. Most are signed by at least one person, usually including a place (probably a hometown) and sometimes a date.

Restoring a Painting that Inspired Willa Cather
1887, 1918, 2017

This 1887 painting of a Russian folktale once hung in the Red Cloud school. The memory of it inspired a scene in Willa Cather's 1918 novel, *My Ántonia*, in which wolves chase a bridal party. But the painting has long been marred by broad tears across its surface. In 2017 the painting was restored at History Nebraska's Gerald R. Ford Conservation Center in Omaha.

Conservator Kenneth Bé faced a difficult challenge. Because of the painting's delicate condition, there was no way to bring the torn, misaligned sections together without causing further damage.

Instead, Bé filled the tears and painted them in. He also painted over the tops of the horses' heads to disguise the misalignment. Carefully documenting the process, he made sure that everything he did can be undone in the future if necessary. Now the painting once again looks like what Willa Cather saw.

Before Restoration

After Restoration

Sod House Family

Lincoln County, circa 1930s

The sod house era isn't as long ago as you might think. Based on clothing styles, this Lincoln County photo appears to be from the 1930s. Long after the arrival of railroads and lumberyards, the soddie remained an inexpensive form of housing. Building a good one required skill and planning.

The back of the photo identifies this as the home of W. W. Johnson, thirty miles northwest of North Platte. It says the Johnsons are members of the Field Home Department of the American Sunday School Union. "Mrs. Johnson and children very much interested in Sunday-School lessons."

Rural Free Delivery Postal Wagon

Seward, early 1900s

Rural Free Delivery meant that farm and ranch families could receive mail at home instead of making a long trip into town to check a post office box.

Along with the telephone, RFD removed some of the traditional isolation of farm life. In addition to personal letters, RFD made it easier for rural residents to make purchases through mail-order catalogs from national retailers such as Sears, Roebuck & Co. and Montgomery Ward. People were no longer limited to what their local merchants had in stock.

The RFD movement began in the late nineteenth century. It was generally adopted by the United States Postal Service in 1902.

Nebraska vs. Grand Island College

Lincoln, September 24, 1904

Nebraska scores the first touchdown of the 1904 season. Forward passes: illegal. Helmets: optional. A thousand spectators came to Antelope Field to watch the Cornhuskers rout Grand Island College 72-0. Nebraska fans were used to lopsided games. In 1903 the undefeated Cornhuskers shut out eight of their eleven opponents, and in 1902 they gave up no points at all.

Stop! That Sign's Yellow!

Nehawka, Cass County, 1976

This 1976 photo was apparently taken to document Nehawka's auditorium (now long gone), but it captures another sign of change.

Did you know stop signs were yellow from 1924 to 1954? Before reflective paint, yellow was more visible at night, and available red pigments tended to fade quickly. After the change to red, some of the old yellow signs stood for many years in out-of-the-way places.

Negro Motorist Green Book

1962

The motion picture *Green Book* won three Academy Awards in 2018, including Best Picture. Its title comes from the *Negro Motorist Green Book*, published under similar titles from 1936 to 1966. The annual booklet was a guide for traveling while Black in Jim Crow America.

The movie is set in 1962. Here is Nebraska's section in that year's edition. These weren't necessarily the only businesses willing to serve non-White travelers, but segregation was real in Nebraska. In 1963, for example, local civil rights groups began a series of boycotts against Omaha businesses that refused to serve Black customers. Such discrimination was illegal under Nebraska law, but the law was meaningless when prosecutors and police failed to enforce it.

NEBRASKA

Hotels — Motels — Tourist Homes — Restaurants

AINSWORTH
Midwest Hotel
Skinner's Cabins

CHARDRON
Oak's Court Motel .... West Hwy. 20

FREMONT
Gus Henderson Tourist Home .... 1725 N. Irving Street
Shady Nook Cabins .... P. O. Box 45

LINCOLN
Deluxe Court .... 4433 No. 70th Street
Lincoln Hotel .... 9th & "P" Streets

OMAHA
Broadview Hotel .... 2060 N. 19th Street
G. H. Ashby Tourist Home .... 2228 Willis Avenue
L. Strawther Tourist Home .... 2220 Willis Avenue
Patton's Hotel .... 2425 Erskine Street
Willis Hotel .... 22nd & Willis

SCOTTSBLUFF
Eagle's Restaurant .... 1603 Broadway
Welsh Roome Hotel .... 1015 9th Avenue

SIDNEY
Long Pine Court .... 1701 Illinois

VALENTINE
Hotel Marion

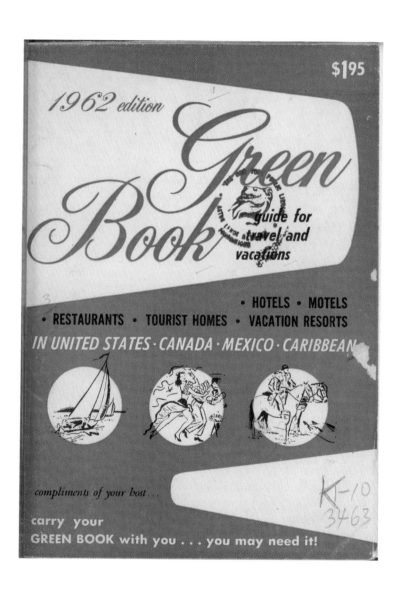

$1⁹⁵

1962 edition

Green Book

guide for travel and vacations

• HOTELS • MOTELS
• RESTAURANTS • TOURIST HOMES • VACATION RESORTS

IN UNITED STATES · CANADA · MEXICO · CARIBBEAN

compliments of your host...

carry your GREEN BOOK with you ... you may need it!

Electric Washing Machine

Kearney, May 1936

This is a photo of hard times that just got a little easier. Bronx native Arthur Rothstein was only twenty years old when he traveled to Nebraska as a photographer for the federal government's Resettlement Administration. The RA was a New Deal agency that relocated unemployed rural and urban families to planned cooperative communities. In addition to economic depression, the Great Plains was suffering from a severe multi-year drought.

Rothstein labeled this photo, "Wife of a farmstead farmer." She is doing laundry with an early electric washing machine. Electricity reduced a woman's daily toil, but town women enjoyed it decades before it was common in rural areas. Senator George Norris's 1936 Rural Electrification Act provided federal support.

Even so, local projects took years to develop. Most farms in Buffalo County had REA power by the early 1950s. By 1949, Nebraska became the nation's only state served entirely by public power.

Girls' Basketball Team
Blue Springs, Gage County, 1924

It isn't clear which championship Blue Springs High School won, but the team and coach posed for a series of photos. Here, no one is ready for the camera, and the image feels contemporary in its informality.

In 1924 the Nebraska High School Athletic Association voted to abolish the girls state basketball tournament and to bar girls' teams from entering any state, district, or county tournaments in the future. Association members voiced "protests against girls' competitive athletics in general."

This was part of a long national backlash against women's sports. The University of Nebraska had already disbanded its women's basketball team after the 1908 season. Physical recreation was OK, but highly competitive, "mannish" play was said to be inappropriate and even harmful to women.

Cornhusker women's basketball returned as a varsity sport in 1974. The girls' state high school basketball tournament resumed in 1977.

Missouri River Flood

Omaha, April 16, 1952

The camera looks upstream from the Douglas Street Bridge toward the Asarco Lead Refinery (now Lewis and Clark Landing). The river was rising.

Some 28,000 volunteers worked day and night to raise existing levees and floodwalls, hauling sandbags in the rain. The river crested two days after this photo.

"The water was sixteen feet higher than the land and up to eighteen inches on the sandbags," wrote B.F. Sylvester for *Nebraska History Magazine*. "Volunteers and Fifth Army soldiers went along raising the levee one bag at a time."

Omaha's barriers held, but other river cities weren't so fortunate. Flood control was one reason the US Army Corps of Engineers was building a chain of dams and reservoirs from Montana to northeast Nebraska. But the "Pick-Sloan Plan" wasn't complete in 1952.

Despite the dams, the Missouri Valley remains vulnerable to extreme floods, more so as the climate warms.

A Pledge Not to Drink

Nebraska City, circa 1877-87

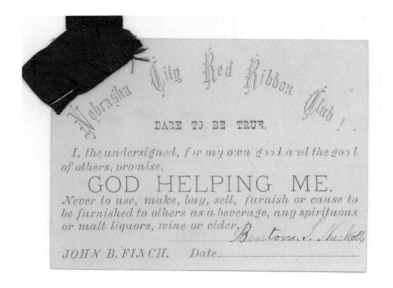

Nebraska City Red Ribbon Club!

DARE TO BE TRUE.

I, the undersigned, for my own good and the good of others, promise,

GOD HELPING ME,

Never to use, make, buy, sell, furnish or cause to be furnished to others as a beverage, any spirituous or malt liquors, wine or cider.

Benton L. Nicholls

JOHN B. FINCH.   Date

Before the Prohibition Era, numerous "temperance" societies encouraged people to give up alcohol "for my own good and the good of others." Members signed pledge cards and wore colored ribbons as badges.

The Red Ribbon Club came to Nebraska in October 1877 when speaker John Finch launched a two-week campaign in Nebraska City. More than 1,600 people signed pledge cards like this one. Finch then organized clubs across the state. By 1888 the Lincoln club was reported to have 16,000 pledge signers.

Many women joined temperance societies in an effort to reduce domestic violence and poverty. Many of the same women became involved in the women's suffrage movement.

The Red Ribbon Club stressed personal reform but soon became involved in politics. Over time it was superseded by overtly political groups such as the Prohibition Party and the Anti-Saloon League.

Earliest Known Photo of African Americans in Nebraska

Brownville, 1864

Nebraska Territory had a small Black population. Slavery was legal here. The 1860 census recorded 81 Black residents, of whom 15 were enslaved. The legislature overrode the governor's veto to abolish slavery in January 1861.

Nebraska's Black population grew after Reconstruction and again during the Great Migration of the early twentieth century. In both eras, Southern African Americans fled racial terrorism and an ever-more-restrictive caste system.

Nebraska had Black homesteaders and cowboys, the Black town of Dewitty in the Sandhills, and extensive Black communities in Omaha, Lincoln, and Nebraska City. The Omaha community grew rapidly during World War I.

Though less blatant than its Southern counterpart, Nebraska's racial caste system marred every aspect of life, limiting access to housing, jobs, education, and legal justice. For many years—and up to the present—the story has usually involved Black Nebraskans challenging longstanding inequalities in opposition to those who say it isn't about race.

First State Capitol

Lincoln, 1869

When it was named the state capital in 1867, the town of Lancaster boasted two stores, a shoe shop, six or seven houses, and about thirty residents. Forces opposed to removing the capital from Omaha now focused their invective on the newly renamed "city" of Lincoln.

"It is founded on fiat," one newspaper complained, "no river, no railroad, no steam wagon, nothing. It is destined for isolation and ultimate oblivion."

Governor David Butler feared that unless a new capitol was completed and ready to receive the state legislature in January 1869, Lincoln would lose its status and the plan for capital removal would fail after all. The builders met their deadline, but the rush-job capitol was so poorly built that it needed to be replaced just twenty years later.

The replacement was bigger but not much better. It too was eventually replaced. Completed in 1934, today's capitol is the third building constructed on the same site.

White Horse Ranch

Near Naper, Boyd County, 1953

They called their new breed of horse "American Albino."

Brothers Cal and Hudson Thompson of West Point began developing the breed in 1917. In 1938 Cal and his wife, Ruth, moved to a 2,400-acre ranch near Naper. They called it El Rancho del Caballo Blanco, but most knew it by its English name, White Horse Ranch.

Training horses and riders, Cal and Ruth's troupes performed at horse shows, fairs, and rodeos until Cal's death in 1963. White Horse Ranch is listed on the National Register of Historic Places.

The Army's Best Horsemen

Fort Robinson, circa 1940

"Thru These Portals Pass the Army's Best Horsemen," reads a sign above a barracks doorway at Fort Robinson, Nebraska. But one doesn't train a horse without some, ah, awkward moments along the way. The best one can hope for is that a photographer isn't standing nearby when the inevitable happens.

The fort began in 1874 as Camp Robinson and served as a cavalry outpost from the Indian Wars up until World War I, when the fort was virtually abandoned. After the war the fort took on a new role as the army's quartermaster remount depot, processing horses and mules for the cavalry and artillery. With opportunities for riding (even polo matches!), it was considered a plum assignment to be stationed at Fort Robinson during those years.

These days the fort is a state historical park. The adobe-brick officers' quarters—visible here across the parade ground—are in high demand as guesthouses for vacationers.

Ladies Ward, State Hospital for the Insane

Norfolk, undated

The hospital now known as the Norfolk Regional Center opened in 1888. It was built to ease overcrowding at the Nebraska Asylum for the Insane in Lincoln. In the early years it had a farm and dairy where many of its inmates (as they were called) worked to raise their own food.

Nationally, such institutions tried to improve their image following *New York World* journalist Nellie Bly's 1887 exposé, *Ten Days in a Madhouse*.

1870s Omaha Skyline

Looking northwest from 15th and Farnam

Omaha thrived despite the loss of the capital to Lincoln. A railroad town, it grew to 16,000 residents by 1870, and doubled in size by 1880.

Here, what is now downtown Omaha is still mostly a mix of wood-frame commercial and residential properties and muddy streets—all without water or sewer systems. The hilly streets were steeper then, too—by the 1920s, men with earthmoving equipment lowered the crest of the hill by as much as 30 feet in places.

The city's first high school, built in 1872, stands atop the former Capitol Hill—site of today's Central High School.

Cowboy Grave Marker

Cherry County, 1879

"IN MEMORY of James Williamson, KILLED BY INDI-ANS, MAY 5, 1879. AGED 28 YEARS."

Violence between cowboys and Indians was a staple of twentieth century Western movies. Hollywood legend greatly exaggerated reality, and unfairly stereotyped indigenous peoples as the usual aggressor.

But acts of violence did happen on the open range. James Williamson was killed near the Snake River by what were said to be Brulé Sioux from Spotted Tail's Rosebud Reservation. Williamson worked on D. J. McCann's Niobrara River ranch southwest of Valentine. Fellow cowboy Louis J. F. "Billy the Bear" Iager carved this headboard with a knife and hot iron. A marble headstone later replaced this marker, which is now in the collections of History Nebraska.

Below right, "Billy the Bear" Iager with an unidentified friend sometime prior to the January 1883 blizzard that cost Iager his fingers and lower legs.

Death of Crazy Horse

Camp Robinson, September 5, 1877

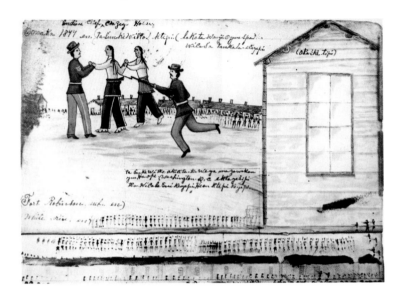

Lakota tribal historian Amos Bad Heart Bull (circa 1868-1913) made this picture in a ledger book.

When gold was discovered in the Black Hills, the US first tried to buy the land from the Lakotas, and then waged war on them when they refused to sell.

The Lakotas, along with Northern Cheyenne and Arapahoes, famously defeated Custer at the Little Bighorn in 1876, but the war went on. By attacking Indian encampments and destroying food and supplies, the army forced one band after another to surrender.

Crazy Horse surrendered in May 1877. "I want this peace to last forever," he told one of the officers, but he was feared by the army and was later betrayed by rivals. A stone marker at Fort Robinson State Park stands near the spot where he was bayoneted by a soldier while resisting arrest. It is often adorned with bundles of sage left by Native people who come to honor his memory.

Red Cross Day

Wahoo, July 4, 1918

During World War I, Wahoo residents raised $60,000 through an auction and fund drives. They boasted that Red Cross Day was "a celebration that can be heard in Berlin." Many Nebraskans "did their bit" by supporting the Red Cross, buying war bonds, and observing "meatless" and "wheatless" days.

Saunders County was typical of Nebraska as a whole. Many local men enlisted in the armed forces, and eighteen of the county's men died in the war. Volunteer projects included making surgical dressings and raising money through four Liberty Loan campaigns.

Nebraska's home front had a darker side as well. The Nebraska Council of Defense harassed people accused of not supporting the war effort, and vigilantes sometimes splashed yellow paint on houses. The state's many German-speakers fell under suspicion, and in 1919 the state legislature banned the teaching of foreign languages to schoolchildren—a law later ruled unconstitutional by the US Supreme Court.

Savidge Brothers

Ewing, Holt County, 1912

John, Joe, George, and Matt Savidge posed for this photo a year after their first powered flight. At the time it wasn't clear that aviation would ever be more than a dangerous stunt.

Two years earlier, the Baysdorfer brothers of Omaha made the first flight in a Nebraska-built airplane near Waterloo. Though the Savidges weren't the first Nebraskan aviators, they were among the first and became well-known as they made public flights in numerous Nebraska communities. Their sister, Mary, was probably the first female in Nebraska to be an airplane passenger.

Matt Savidge learned to loop the plane, and was apparently the world's first pilot to do skywriting. He died in a crash in 1916, after which his brothers gave up aviation.

US Airmail at Offutt Field

Bellevue, circa 1926-29

Regular airmail service began in Nebraska in 1920, with cross-country flights stopping in North Platte and Omaha. Ak-Sar-Ben Field served as Omaha's first airfield, but in 1924 the US Air Mail relocated to the new Offutt Field at Fort Crook. The army did little flying in those days, so the field (and it was literally a field) wasn't busy.

The first airmail planes were converted World War I bombers, but what we see here is a Douglas M-2, designed specifically for airmail in 1926. It would have looked big and powerful to anyone who saw it then.

A passenger sits in the front cockpit, which was normally enclosed as a mail compartment. As with many biplanes of the period, the pilot sat in the rear cockpit for reasons of balance and visibility. In this case, it's all for the camera—this plane isn't going anywhere without its propeller.

Martin Bomber Plant

Bellevue, circa 1942

Bellevue had fewer than 1,200 residents in 1940. A December 6 announcement changed everything: The Glenn L. Martin Company would build a bomber plant here.

The announcement came a year and a day before Pearl Harbor, but the US was well into the war by the time the plant's first B-26 "Marauder" took to the air on August 11, 1942. Factory employees lined the runway to watch. Some even came in on their day off.

That may be the event shown in the unlabeled photo at right. The sign reads: "Omaha. The B26. One Victory Won, Greater Victories to Come."

The plant was huge. The assembly building shown here covers 1.7 million square feet, and the new runway was two miles long. The plant switched to B-29 assembly in 1944. The facilities later became the heart of Offutt Air Force Base and the Strategic Air Command. The runway was finally replaced in 2021.

Robert Kennedy "Whistle-Stop" Campaign

Lexington, Nebraska, April 28, 1968

RFK's speech was part of a whistle-stop campaign tour from Omaha to Cheyenne. Few states had presidential primaries in 1968, and Nebraska's May 14 primary was a big deal. Kennedy won Nebraska and three other states before his assassination on June 5.

On the Republican side, Richard Nixon's decisive Nebraska victory made his nomination seem inevitable. Ronald Reagan didn't campaign here, but his surprisingly strong showing pointed toward the future.

For many years it was considered undignified for a presidential candidate to campaign on his own behalf. Nebraskan William Jennings Bryan broke with tradition in 1896 by going on a nationwide tour. In the twentieth century, the whistle-stop tour, with short speeches from the back of a railcar, became a tradition for sitting presidents and hopefuls alike. But after 1968 the decline of passenger rail travel made it a thing of the past.

Hall County Courthouse

Grand Island, built in 1904, shown in 1913 postcard

Hall County Court House, Grand Island, Neb.
On line of Union Pacific.

The Hall County Courthouse is a Grand Island landmark. Built in 1901-04 of limestone with brick accents, it's an outstanding example of Beaux-Arts architecture.

Beaux-Arts is a style seen in nationally known early twentieth century buildings such as New York City's Grand Central Terminal and the New York Public Library. The old Beatrice City Library is another local example, but the style is rare in Nebraska.

This courthouse shares some history with the Spanish Renaissance Revival-style St. Cecilia's Cathedral in Omaha. It is also linked to the tiny Keystone Community Church, which has Catholic and Protestant altars at either end, and reversible pews. Also part of the story are the elegant plaster-and-lath buildings that stood briefly at Omaha's Trans-Mississippi and International Exposition in 1898. What is the connection?

All were designed by Thomas R. Kimball of Omaha. A master of multiple styles, Kimball is thus far the only architect in the Nebraska Hall of Fame.

Before a Women's Suffrage Parade

Blair, July 11, 1914

Women tried and failed for decades to gain the right to vote. At times victory seemed so close. Nebraska could have been the first territory to allow women the vote. In 1856 a suffrage bill passed in the lower house of the territorial legislature, but it failed in the upper house. (Wyoming Territory gave women the vote in 1869.)

Nebraska became the second state to allow women to vote in school district elections, but Nebraska's all-male voters rejected women's wider suffrage in 1882, 1891, and 1914—the year of this photo. A limited-suffrage act passed in 1917. It would have allowed women to vote in some elections, but court challenges delayed it until the Nineteenth Amendment in 1920 made it moot.

Niobrara on Wheels

Knox County, 1881

The town of Niobrara has had three locations in 162 years. It was founded in 1857 along the Missouri River near its confluence with the Niobrara River.

In March 1881 an ice jam flooded the town with three to six feet of water. By April Niobrara had been flooded three times. Residents had had enough. They decided to move the town, building by building, to higher ground. Teamsters used house jacks, winches and capstans, block-and-tackles, oxen, mules, and horses. The new site was a mile-and-a-half to the southwest.

All was well until the early 1970s, when the water table began rising behind Gavins Point Dam. Niobrara was moved again. The third Niobrara was dedicated on July 4, 1977.

In 2019 yet another major flood devastated businesses on lower ground, but most of the town—including its residential neighborhood—was high and dry.

Prohibition Raid

Omaha, circa 1922

Douglas County sheriffs pose with materials from an illegal still. Statewide prohibition took effect in May 1917, two years ahead of national prohibition. Illegal manufacture and sale of alcohol continued, creating a need for secrecy.

These men were proud to show themselves doing their jobs, but the larger story is all the local stills that were left alone. In Omaha, many small-time offenders were arrested even as larger bootleggers thrived under the protection of crime boss Tom Dennison and corrupt local officials.

National prohibition ended in December 1933. Nebraskans voted to end statewide prohibition in November 1934.

How to Cross the Platte River

Fort Kearny, 1866

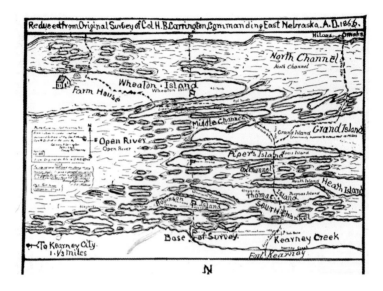

How difficult was it to cross the Platte River without a bridge? This 1866 map gives you some idea. The river was notorious for its braided channel and patches of quicksand. The map shows the best places to ford.

But some things are confusing. What is Kearney City (lower-left) doing south of the river and west of the fort? And how is Grand Island north of the fort?

Kearney City—also called Dobytown for its adobe buildings—was described by an 1860 visitor as a "gambling hell" populated by "as bad a crowd of men and women as ever got together on the plains." The present city of Kearney was founded in 1872 north of the river.

Grand Island, meanwhile, was a long island between channels of the Platte. It was named "La Grande Isle" by eighteenth century French traders. The city originally known as Grand Island Station was founded the year this map was drawn, but well to the east.

Mexican Immigrant Mother and Children

Omaha, August 15, 1922

A mother stands with her children in South Omaha. Dad is probably working a long shift at a nearby packing plant.

Starting in the early twentieth century, and especially during and after World War I, Mexican immigrants came seeking work—to the meatpacking district of South Omaha, the railroad yards of Havelock outside Lincoln, and the farms of Scotts Bluff County.

Writing for *Nebraska History Magazine*, historian Bryan Winston writes: "Railroad workers made boxcars into homes. South Omaha residents often lived as boarders when they "wintered" in the "Magic City" and accepted seasonal employment at the many meatpacking plants. Ethnic Mexicans in Scottsbluff built adobe homes from Nebraskan soil and leftover hay from livestock railroad yards."

Today more than 10 percent of Nebraskans are Latino, a proportion that is expected to continue growing.

Baby May of the Walter Savidge Amusement Co.

Wayne, circa 1910s

Baby May, "America's Fat Girl," was a sideshow attraction for the Walter Savidge traveling circus. The public could walk up the stairs to where she sat on a plush chair, and converse with her in any of the seven languages she spoke.

Based in Wayne, the Savidge circus toured small towns in Nebraska and surrounding states from 1906 to 1941. It was known for providing clean, family-oriented entertainment with acrobats, music, drama, carnival rides, and no risqué shows.

Today we'd use the expression "body shaming" to describe this type of show, but at the time it was considered a family-friendly attraction. "Freak shows" featuring physically unusual people were widespread for many years. They were declining in popularity by the twentieth century and became rare by mid-century.

Gage County Courthouse

Beatrice, 1909 postcard

Gage County was organized in 1856, but lacked a courthouse until about 1870. Twenty years later this grand Richardsonian Romanesque building replaced the first courthouse.

Many Nebraska counties have similar stories. Although frontier courts often met in rented space and early courthouses were usually small and cheaply built, by the late nineteenth century a grand courthouse became a point of pride. Nebraskans were eager to show their progress. The Gage County Courthouse opened in 1892 and is listed on the National Register of Historic Places.

Sandhill Prosperity
Wheeler County, circa 1910

"You ask what place I like the best
The sand hills, O the old sand hills
The place Kinkaiders make their home
And prairie chickens freely roam…

"The corn we raise is our delight
The melons too are out of sight
Potatoes grown are extra fine
And can't be beat in any clime…."
—from "The Kinkaider's Song"

The 1904 Kinkaid Act allowed homesteaders to claim 640 acres of land in much of western Nebraska where smaller farms were impractical, but most of the new "Kinkaiders" had higher hopes than they ever had profits. This John Nelson postcard photo captures some of the humor of the time.

Willa Cather in Beauty and the Beast

Red Cloud Opera House, February 4, 1888

Wearing a top hat and wax mustache, Willa Cather played "The Merchant" (father of Beauty) in J. Barmby's comedic play. The 14-year-old performed her role "with such grace and ease that she called forth the admiration of the entire audience," said the *Red Cloud Chief*. Two years later, Cather moved to Lincoln for a year of Latin school before enrolling at the University of Nebraska.

As an adolescent and as a college student, Cather defied gender expectations, calling herself William, cutting her hair short like a boy's, and frequently dressing in male or androgynous clothing. She aspired to be a medical doctor before turning to writing and becoming one of the nation's most beloved novelists. As an adult Cather dressed conventionally (and stylishly) but wrote some of her best fiction from the perspective of a male protagonist.

Pilger Pagoda

Pilger, Stanton County, circa 1917-1930

A photographer recorded this dilapidated, pagoda-topped building sometime in the mid-twentieth century. What was it doing in Pilger? Did it have anything to do with Nebraska's Japanese immigrant community?

No, it wasn't about immigrant culture. It was about marketing. The building, now gone, was a gas station.

As automobiles became faster and more common, retail businesses invested in billboards, logos, and unusual structures to catch the eye of high-speed passersby. Between 1917 and 1930, Wadhams Oil and Grease Company of Milwaukee built more than 100 pagoda-roofed filling stations across the Midwest. There was no actual Japanese connection. It was simply corporate branding at a time in which Japanese culture was relatively popular in the United States.

William Jennings Bryan Accepts Presidential Nomination

State Capitol, Lincoln, August 12, 1908

Wait—did Lincoln host a Democratic National Convention?

No, the convention that year was in Denver. Nominee William Jennings Bryan didn't attend.

That was normal in 1908. It was still common for presidential nominees not to attend their party's national convention. Bryan awaited the result at home in Lincoln, and delivered his acceptance speech from the north side of the capitol. It was his third nomination.

Bryan carried Nebraska, Colorado, Nevada, and the South, but lost to Republican nominee William Howard Taft. Despite his three electoral losses Bryan remained powerful in the Democratic Party, helping to reshape it along more progressive lines.

Hose Team

Fremont, 1886

Early fire brigades didn't always have teams of horses on hand. Sometimes the quickest way to move hose was with a team of athletic young men. In August 1886 Fremont hosted a four-day statewide firemen's tournament in which thousands of spectators watched hose teams and hook-and-ladder teams compete for cash prizes.

Confronted by a Question of Clothes

Plattsmouth, 1910s

Local businesses have long used parade floats as colorful marketing tools. C. E. Wescott settled in Plattsmouth in 1879 and opened his clothing store soon after. His sons took over the store after he retired in 1906.

Wescott's retail career coincided with a period of rapid growth in the availability of manufactured goods and the amount of advertising used to sell them. By the time of this photo, it wasn't enough to let the public know that you sold certain products. Savvy local merchants followed the lead of the new advertising industry and made their businesses memorable.

According to a 1922 *Plattsmouth Journal* article, Wescott's motto, "One Price and No Monkey Business," "was made famous in all parts of the state."

Engineer Cantonment

Present-day Washington County, 1819

How do you find an archeological site that's been lost for nearly 200 years? In 2003, History Nebraska archeologists made the discovery of a lifetime—and they did it using some surprising tools, including this 1819 watercolor.

The painting shows a place called Engineer Cantonment, winter quarters of the Stephen Long Expedition. Archeologists knew the site was on the west bank of the Missouri River, north of present-day Omaha, but below the site of Fort Atkinson State Historical Park. Cruising the river, they looked at the bluffs until they passed a spot that looked familiar:

Could it be? Using a trenching machine (the kind used for digging cable trenches), they tested the area where the painting shows buildings. They found artifacts that identified the long-lost site. A full archeological excavation followed.

Omaha Legion Airport (Today's Eppley Airfield)
August 8, 1928

By 1928 the airplane was no longer merely a stunt machine—that was the message of this carefully staged photo. The family arriving by night in an Interstate Air Lines Ryan Brougham illustrates the development of commercial aviation.

The public would have noticed the plane's resemblance to Charles Lindbergh's custom-built Ryan, the *Spirit of St. Louis*, which he famously flew from New York to Paris a year earlier. (And visited Omaha and other US cities afterward.) Nebraskans were proud that Lindbergh, a Minnesotan, had taken his first flying lessons in Lincoln in 1922.

Pilot Evelyn Sharp

Ord, May 19, 1938

Evelyn Sharp wasn't Nebraska's first female pilot, but is remembered for all she accomplished during her brief life.

Sharp's father owned a café in Ord and rented rooms. When Sharp was sixteen, one of the boarders was a man who had opened a local flying school. At one point it wasn't going so well, and the man couldn't pay his rent. He offered to teach young Evelyn how to fly.

Sharp moved quickly. She earned her commercial pilot's license when she was eighteen, bought a plane, took up barnstorming, became one of the first female airmail pilots, and became a flight instructor—all by the time she was twenty.

During World War II Sharp rose to squadron commander in the WASPs (Women Airforce Service Pilots), doing non-combat flying. In 1944 the fighter plane she was ferrying lost an engine on takeoff. Sharp was killed in the resulting crash, only twenty-four years old.

"Bulldogging" at Nebraska's Big Rodeo

Burwell, 1951

Burwell
Home of NEBR'S
Big Rodeo

"Dude Smith"
Bulldoggin

Photo
1951

Steers are rarely injured in this event, but the risk to the "bulldogger" is considerable. And look at the man on horseback, dismounting while still in motion, looking back but in complete control as he casually smokes a cigarette.

None of this is unusual for a rodeo. What is noteworthy about the photo is how well it captures its subjects' strength, skill, and teamwork.

Founded in 1921, the Burwell rodeo became known for drawing top talent, such as Texan Vernon "Dude" Smith. Other small-town rodeos across the state drew local and regional competitors—men and women who worked at ranches and feedlots during the week and hitched up their horse trailers on weekends—and still do today.

Buck-A-Roo Motel

Norfolk, circa 1966-70

This postcard hits many of right notes for mid-twentieth century travel: neon, Western iconography, and single-story buildings wrapped around a parking lot.

Motels (a contraction of "motor hotel") made a point of distinguishing themselves from hotels. The Hotel Norfolk had long been the city's main lodging for travelers, but by the mid-1960s the downtown landmark was being converted to apartments. At the Buck-A-Roo, meanwhile, motorists were right on Highway 81 and could park in front of their door.

The sign reveals traveler expectations: air conditioning, telephone, and TV were luxuries worth bragging about—though by this time "Color TV" was becoming the hot new amenity.

The Buck-A-Roo Motel is gone, but the Hotel Norfolk building remains and is listed on the National Register of Historic Places.

Nebraska versus Stanford in the Rose Bowl

Pasadena, California, January 1, 1941

This top-ten matchup was the Cornhuskers' first bowl game and remained a bright spot in Nebraskans' memory during the two decades of gridiron futility that followed. Fans spoke of it with such pride that Coach Bob Devaney used to joke that it took several years after he came here in 1962 to learn that the Cornhuskers actually lost the game.

The game is also considered historically significant to the development of football. Stanford (in white jerseys) capped an undefeated season using an innovative offense called the T formation. To a fan in 1940, it looked strange to see the quarterback—normally a blocking back—standing directly behind the center and taking the snap, with three running backs lined up five yards behind. Stanford's 21-13 victory over the powerful Nebraska team helped convince many coaches that the "T" was superior to the popular single-wing formation.

Pembleton Family Band

York, circa 1889-1895

Musical entertainment was far more localized in the years before recording artists and radio.

Martin Luther Pembleton was a Civil War veteran and drum major in the Nebraska National Guard. Later the father of nine led a fife-and-drum corps known at different times as the Pembleton Family Band, the Pembleton Drum Corps, or Major Pembleton's Baby Drummers. They performed at various events, and were popular at gatherings of the G.A.R. (Grand Army of the Republic, an organization for Union Army Civil War veterans). Even the children were renowned for their skill.

Republican River Flood
McCook, May 31, 1935

RESCUE WORK McCook FLOOD 5-31-35

Nebraska's deadliest flood happened in the middle of a drought. Torrential rains sent a wall of water down the river valley, killing more than a hundred people.

Here, forty men are stranded atop the McCook power plant. A man pulls himself hand over hand toward the building. He is bringing a line so that men can be shuttled to dry land via a telephone cable car. Two men were thus rescued before the water tower collapsed in the rushing water. The other men were rescued by boat the next day after the water began to recede.

This and other floods, plus a desire for irrigation, led the federal government to build a series of dams on the Republican and its tributaries.

Earliest Known Photo of Chimney Rock

1866

Finding a long-lost artifact on eBay was still enough of a novelty in 2009 that the story made headlines when historian John Carter discovered the oldest known photo of Chimney Rock on the internet auction site.

Carter had known that the 1866 Charles Savage photo had once existed, but for many years it was considered lost.

Chimney Rock was the most written-about landmark along the Oregon, Mormon, and California trails, but cameras were bulky, expensive, and fragile during the overland trails era. Savage's photo was made near the end of that era, three years before the completion of the transcontinental railroad began to siphon off traffic bound for Utah or the West Coast.

The photo also shows how Chimney Rock has changed over time. The bottom photo was taken from a similar location 100 years later, in 1966.

Poster from Oscar's Palladium

Sargent, Custer County, circa 1940s

Omaha bandleader Earl Graves was active in the 1940s-1960s, when Omaha was a center for touring African American jazz bands. In Sargent, Oscar's hosted "territory" bands traveling the regional circuit, plus big names such as Lawrence Welk, the Dorsey Brothers, and Guy Lombardo.

Omaha bandleader Preston Love (1921-2004) recalled that Black orchestras adjusted their style to fit the tastes of White audiences. "No matter how good your repertoire was from the standpoint of swinging… you must play at least fifty percent of the music in the Lawrence Welk and Guy Lombardo style to please the dancers in that area."

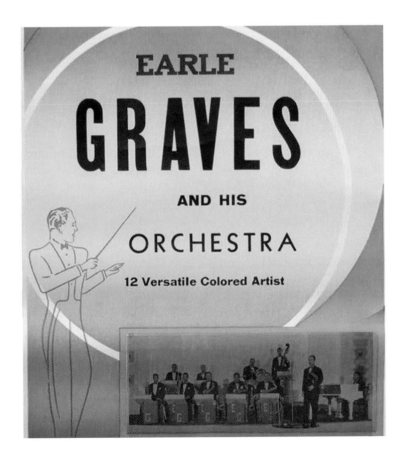

This $3 bill Was Real Money!

DeSoto, Washington County, 1857

Nebraska in the 1850s was a territory full of paper towns and paper money. Hard currency was scarce on the frontier, and chartered but otherwise unregulated "wildcat" banks stepped in to fill an economic need for cash.

This 1857 three-dollar bill was real money as long as people had confidence in the DeSoto, Nebraska, bank that issued it. If the bank was suspect, the bill would trade at well below par; when the bank failed later that year, the bill became worthless. A nationwide financial crash known as the Panic of 1857 wiped out speculative banks and towns alike.

Shoe Repair Shop

North Platte, 1934

When was the last time you had shoes repaired?

You may have your cowboy boots re-soled, but most modern shoes aren't made with the expectation of repair. They go from store to closet to landfill.

How expensive were shoes in the 1930s? A quick search of Nebraska newspaper ads for October 1934 shows women's shoes mostly in the $5-to-$7 range ($93 to $130 today), with some as high as $12.75 ($237.28). Men's were $2.39-$5.00 ($44-$93). The 1934 Sears catalog had shoes for less, with women's starting at $1.49 ($27.73) and men's starting at $3.45 ($64.20).

During the Great Depression, new shoes or even the services of the local repair shop were out of reach for families of the unemployed. Children might go barefoot in the summer, and old shoes were lined with cardboard to cover holes.

Old and New Locomotives

York, September 26, 1928

No one could miss the message of the 1887 and 1922 locomotives arranged side by side for the York County Homecoming Celebration. York itself was not yet sixty years old, and older residents remembered the county as frontier. The celebration recognized how much had changed in one lifetime.

As for the locomotives, both were still in service on the Chicago, Burlington and Quincy Railroad. The one on the left had been rebuilt at the Havelock shops in 1918. A relic of an earlier time, it remained in service until 1933. The big engine on the right was scrapped in 1953 during the transition from steam to diesel.

Movie Night at Orthopedic Hospital

Lincoln, April 18, 1940

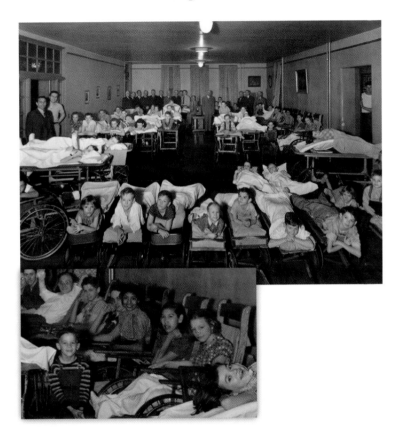

The Nebraska Orthopedic Hospital was founded in 1905. It was the state's first effort to provide services for children with musculoskeletal conditions, many of whom lived in appalling conditions in county poor houses at the turn of the twentieth century.

Located at 11th and South streets in Lincoln, the NOH closed in 1971 and its responsibilities were transferred to the University of Nebraska Medical Center in Omaha.

Wedding Dress
Norfolk, 1886

Emma Bell's sister designed this silk taffeta bustle dress, and Emma wore it when she married Harry Hardy in Norfolk on November 16, 1886. (The tradition of white wedding dresses, worn only once, is relatively recent.)

Snow was falling as the newlyweds boarded a Union Pacific train. They were bound for their honeymoon in Omaha, but the weather worsened as the train headed south. Emma and Harry decided to get off at Richland. Emma's brother-in-law was the railroad agent there, and he and his family lived in the depot.

They were all snowbound there for three days. Emma took over the household duties since her sister was stranded in Norfolk where she had gone for the wedding. The dress and the story are now in the collections of the Nebraska History Museum.

Pawnshops on Lower Douglas Street

Omaha, November 1938

Omaha's warehouse district ("Jobbers Canyon") drew a transient population of unskilled laborers. Nearby Douglas Street became known for its pawnshops, lodging houses, cheap restaurants, employment agencies, and labor halls. It was part of the larger story of hobos in Nebraska.

Photographer John Vachon visited Omaha in October and November 1938 to take photos for the US government's Farm Security Administration. Partly as a way to build support for the New Deal, the agency created a nationwide pictorial record of the Great Depression.

Grade School Classroom

Fairmont, circa 1890

Wouldn't you like to be a student in this classroom?

This old photo looks curiously modern on closer inspection. From the professional-looking chalk art, to the pump organ, bird pictures, dollhouse and model farm, the teacher demonstrates creativity and an artistic bent.

But this was an exceptional classroom. Most schools were poorly funded, and many were taught by teenagers who had only an eighth-grade education themselves. In 1890, fewer than 5 percent of Americans graduated from high school, and students averaged fewer than 90 days of school attendance per year. Thirteen percent of Americans over age 14 were illiterate, and the rate of functional illiteracy was probably much higher.

Someone was proud enough of this classroom to photograph it. It represented an ideal that a growing number of parents wanted for their children.

Gering's First Trees

April 24, 1936

Photographer and naturalist Frank Shoemaker took this photo in Gering on Arbor Day, 1936. Someone told him that these two hackberries were the first trees planted in the newly established town back in 1887. They stood at the corner of 10th and M Streets next to Dutton Implement.

It says something when people remember the planting of particular trees almost fifty years later, or that such modest specimens could reign as the grand old trees of a city. Much of Nebraska was so sparsely timbered that individual trees once served as landmarks—such as the Lone Tree of Central City or the Lone Willow of Gordon.

Downtown Gretna

Early 1900s

Wait – Gretna has a downtown? While today most retail business happens at the outlet mall along I-80, Gretna's old business district centers on Angus Street and McKenna Avenue. The buildings shown here are gone, but McKenna still has its brick pavement, which apparently was about to be laid when this photo was taken.

Incorporated in 1889, Gretna is a relatively new town by eastern Nebraska standards. Nearby Forest City had existed since 1856, but was doomed in 1886 when it was left off the Burlington Railroad between Omaha and Ashland. Gretna was platted that same year.

Junior KKK Membership Application

Saunders County, 1920s

Form J-44

No.

APPLICATION FOR MEMBERSHIP

JUNIOR KU KLUX KLAN

Name.. Age.................

(Surname)   (Christian Name)

Address ....

Parent's Name ....

Parent's Religious Affiliations...

(Church)

Applicant's Sunday School ....

Occupation... Tel. No. ....

In making this application I wish to state on my "*HONOR*" that I am a Native-born, White, Gentile, Protestant American Boy and that I believe in the tenets and Principles of the Knights of the Ku Klux Klan and that, if elected to membership, I will strive to so live that my life will be an example to Americans everywhere; furthermore, that my parents or guardians have consented to this application.

Date .... 192....

                                                                (Signature of Applicant)

Endorser ....

Endorser ....

There was a time when the Ku Klux Klan and its openly White supremacist beliefs were mainstream. In the 1920s the Klan was a nationwide organization with a women's auxiliary and children's programs. Most of its paid speakers were Protestant ministers. At its peak, the KKK claimed 45,000 "Native-born, White, Gentile, Protestant" members in Nebraska. The white hoods were for group identity and intimidation. Members did not need to conceal their identity.

In addition to White supremacy, the Klan stood for nativism, anti-Catholicism, and anti-Semitism. It successfully backed the Immigration Act of 1924 to restrict immigration from non-Western European countries. The Klan also supported Prohibition and portrayed itself as a patriotic, Christian organization that stood for traditional morality, "an example to Americans everywhere."

Behlen Atomic Test Building

Columbus, May 5, 1955

Walt Behlen of Columbus faced a challenge in convincing farmers that his corrugated steel buildings were sturdy even without internal frames.

This one survived an atomic bomb.

At a nuclear test site in Nevada, this building withstood a thirty-kiloton blast from 6,800 feet away, enduring pressure loads of 600 pounds per square foot with only minor damage. It was reassembled outside the Behlen Manufacturing facility in Columbus, where it was painted "atomic orange" in honor of the feat. A second Behlen building from the blast site is displayed at the University of Nebraska-Lincoln East Campus.

Cars and Pedestrians in Downtown Omaha

1920s

Does the street belong to cars or pedestrians?

Urban streets used to be open spaces shared by wagons, street railways, and pedestrians, who were not restricted to sidewalks.

Pedestrian fatalities mounted as automobiles became faster and more numerous. Facing public backlash in the 1920s, the auto industry launched a nationwide public relations campaign to redefine the term "jaywalking." "Jay" was a slang term similar to "hick" or "rube," and a "jaywalker" was the sort of bumpkin who lacked urban sidewalk etiquette. The PR campaign shifted the word's usage to ridicule pedestrians who strayed off the sidewalk except at intersections.

This photo looks west along Douglas from 16th Street. The familiar Brandeis building is on the left. A traffic cop directs cars but not pedestrians, who cross Omaha's busiest intersection at will.

But we see no jaywalkers.

Mike Shonsey's Cattle War Rifle

Merrick County, circa 1893

Mike Shonsey was a marked man when he fled to Nebraska in 1893.

The ranch foreman had killed at least one man, maybe more, during Wyoming's 1892 Johnson County "cattle war." Cattle barons affiliated with the Wyoming Stock Growers Association tried to kill or drive out small ranch operators who were moving onto the ranges where the big companies ran their herds. The barons said employees like Shonsey were only targeting rustlers.

Shonsey worked for cattleman Thomas B. Hord in Central City and Clarks, and became a partner in several Hord enterprises. Hord was a pioneer of the modern cattle industry, with large-scale feeding operations that used science-based methods. Shonsey's photo may be iconic of the open-range era, but he spent most of his career as a modern cattleman.

In 2016 Shonsey's great-grandson, also named Mike Shonsey, donated the Winchester Model 1886 carbine shown in both photos to the Nebraska History Museum.

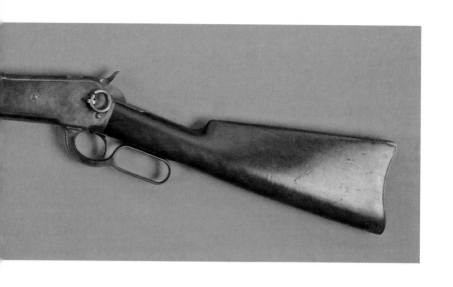

Town of Omadi "Extinct in Missouri River"

Dakota County

It wasn't a flood that swallowed Omadi, Nebraska. It was simply the meandering Missouri River doing what the river had always done.

This badge was worn in 1919 at the Annual Reunion of the Pioneers & Old Settlers Association of Dakota County, Nebraska. By then, only old-timers remembered how Omadi was founded in 1856, how it boasted a schoolhouse and two sawmills, the first hotel and first newspaper in Dakota County, and the first lumberyard on the upper Missouri. Steamboats from St. Louis used to deliver cargo, and people talked of making Omadi the county seat.

But Omadi was built on the outside of a river bend, where the channel kept eroding the cut banks. Residents began removing houses and buildings in 1858. The river covered the entire site by 1865.

Omadi is gone, but a local name survives. Charles Rouleau had been the site's first Euroamerican settler. He moved downstream and became the namesake of the phonetically-spelled town of Rulo.

Rocking Chair

Plattsmouth, 1858

Thomas Mitchell (1811-1900) is said to have made this rocking chair in Plattsmouth in 1858, a year after he moved to Nebraska Territory from Ohio. He set out when Nebraska was still booming with land speculators—people looking to flip land claims or town lots for a quick profit before heading back east.

Then a nationwide financial meltdown known as the "Panic of 1857" wiped out speculators and many fledgling towns besides. Plattsmouth was one of the survivors.

By the time Mitchell was turning these chair legs and spindles on his lathe, most of the people remaining in Plattsmouth were actual settlers who intended to stick it out. (Or else they were too broke to move away!)

Jane and Thomas Mitchell's seventh child was born that year. Jane died three years later. Thomas lived to be 88, dying in Plattsmouth in 1900. The chair was later donated to History Nebraska.

Telephone Office and Outhouse

Maxwell, Lincoln County, early 1900s

The Maxwell and Brady Telephone Company incorporated on May 1, 1901, with eight local shareholders and $2,000 in capital. By 1916 it had 154 telephones on its exchange.

Here's the exchange building, with a rickety wooden walkway out front and what looks like an outhouse out back. The company's customers were mostly business owners and well-to-do residents more likely to have indoor plumbing, but the "water closet" didn't always precede the telephone.

If they had wired up a phone in the outhouse, now that would be modern.

Susan B. Anthony and the Abbott Sisters
Grand Island, 1881-82

Long before Grace and Edith Abbott defined social work in the twentieth century, their suffragist parents hosted Susan B. Anthony during an 1882 Nebraska referendum campaign. Anthony was hopeful that Nebraska men would extend voting rights to women.

Anthony wrote to Elizabeth Abbott on August 22, 1881, calling her "My Dear 'Little Boss.'" Though she always looks severe in her photos, Anthony's letter is upbeat and enthusiastic.

"It is our duty as the National Mother to put all our forces in Nebraska" in hopes of victory, she wrote, and "what a triumph it would be!!"

Anthony stayed with the Abbotts while campaigning in Grand Island. She shared a bed with six-year-old Edith, who was mightily proud of her association with the great "Miss Anthony."

Hay on a Truck

Bancroft, circa 1935

We're not saying this is the best way to move hay, but it can be done.

Farmers commonly use heavy-duty trucks, but what is meant by "heavy-duty" has changed over the years. Under all that hay is a 1934 or 1935 Chevrolet/GMC 1.5 ton truck. It had dual rear wheels and was powered by a 207-cubic-inch six-cylinder engine, which produced a whopping 68 horsepower.

This 2015 Smart car has 70 horsepower.

Granted, those old trucks were geared low enough to have a lot of torque. And this little car's suspension wouldn't support a load of hay. Still, it's amazing how much work farmers got done with trucks that today's drivers would consider ridiculously underpowered.

Laundry Workers

Crete, 1909

No child labor laws protected the little girl shown here.

Chartered by Congress in 1907, the National Child Labor Committee proposed state legislation, but change was slow. Many Americans opposed government regulation, and low-income families needed the extra income even if it kept their children out of school.

In 1923, the NCLC reported that more than half of the contract beet laborers in Nebraska's North Platte Valley were under age 16. Nearly a third were under age 10. Most were children of immigrants.

Children's rights advocates didn't give up. The same year as this photo, a young woman from Grand Island, Grace Abbott, earned a master's degree in political science from the University of Chicago. Abbott wrote extensively about the exploitation of immigrants, and campaigned for federal laws protecting children's rights. She expanded child labor regulations as head of the US Department of Labor's Children's Bureau from 1921 to 1934, and continued to advocate for child welfare until her death in 1939.

Elvis Fans at Omaha Civic Auditorium

May 20, 1956

Why is this young man all shook up? Elvis Presley performed at the University of Nebraska Coliseum on May 19, 1956, and at the Omaha Civic Auditorium the next day. This photo of Omaha fans made the front page of the *World-Herald*. You can see how the photo has been touched up in pencil for better reproduction on newsprint.

"What's happened to our teenagers? Are their morals and standards so low that they have to watch this Elvis Presley perform his downright immoral and filthy actions?" asked the writer of a *World-Herald* "Public Pulse" letter.

Others defended Elvis.

"Remember Grandma, Rudy Valentino, and the gals who went into hysterics over him. Mom, too," one person wrote, referring to a star of the silent film era. Another writer asked,

"What are teen-agers expected to do? Sit and listen to Chopin?"

Presley returned to Omaha in 1974 and 1977. His show at the Civic Auditorium on June 19, 1977, was one of his final performances and aired as a TV special after his death later that year.

Jumpin' with Gold's

Lincoln, 1957

"Things were really 'jumpin' at Cotner Terrace last Monday evening," reported *Gold Tips*, the Gold's employee newsletter, on May 11, 1957. The longtime downtown Lincoln retailer had a 15-Year Club into which employees were initiated after fifteen years with the company.

The circus-themed 1957 banquet honored nineteen employees, who were "full of vim and vigor and had the Initiating Committee thoroughly 'bushed' before the evening was over." Even better, "the entertainment committee . . . arranged a Rock'n Roll program which had clubbers jumpin' and squealing."

Scribner Tornado

Dodge County, May 24, 1902

Five distinct funnel clouds appeared above Scribner in less than an hour. When the storm arose, main street was busy with local families in town for their Saturday shopping.

Those who didn't run for the nearest cellar marveled at the shape of the twisters. The *Lincoln Journal* described them as small, with a "light, feathery appearance against the black cloud area" and with "the 'tails' extending and lowering until they seemed a half mile or more in length, twisting and knotting in an amazing manner."

At least one of the five touched down nearby, damaging three farms but sparing the town. This photo later appeared in the April 1908 issue of *Popular Mechanics* magazine.

Wind Wagon at Fort Kearny

May 27, 1860

You've got to give these guys points for creativity. Samuel Peppard's wind ship was designed to carry freight without a team of mules. A trial run from Oskaloosa, Kansas, followed the Oregon Trail to Fort Kearny, Nebraska, and then headed toward Denver.

The wagon required a favorable wind and was difficult to control, but it could reach speeds of up to 15 miles per hour. Three weeks into the journey, a tornado wrecked the wagon about a hundred miles from Denver.

This illustration, "The Wind Ship of the Prairies: Fort Kearney, May 27, 1860," appeared in *Frank Leslie's Illustrated Newspaper*.

Construction of the Spillway Tower

Kingsley Dam, Keith County, December 21, 1937

The world's second largest hydraulic-fill dam when constructed, Kingsley was built by pumping sand from the riverbed. Loess clay formed the dam's watertight core. The spillway began generating electricity in 1941. Lake C. W. McConaughy was providing irrigation water through more than 500 miles of canals and laterals of the "Tri-County Project" a few years later. The dam and lake are named for two early promoters: Minden banker George P. Kingsley and grain merchant and Holdrege mayor C. W. McConaughy.

Dr. Susan La Flesche Picotte

Walthill Hospital, Thurston County, circa 1890s-1900s

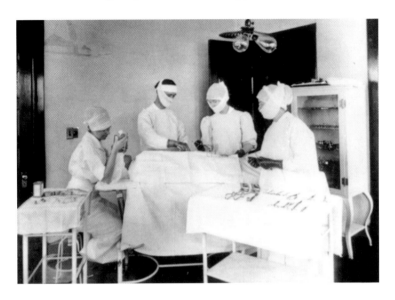

We conclude with a rare turn-of-the-twentieth-century view of an all-female medical staff in an operating room. Where was this progressive hospital? In tiny Walthill on the Omaha Indian Reservation. The photo is not labeled with names of individuals, but the attending physician (second from left) can be none other than Dr. Susan La Flesche Picotte, the youngest daughter of Omaha Chief "Iron Eye" (Joseph La Flesche). In 1889 Picotte became the first Native American to earn a medical degree. She practiced medicine in Walthill and in Bancroft. She was also a strong public advocate for the Omaha people, and raised money to build a hospital in Walthill. The building is now a National Historic Landmark.

Photo Credits

Photos are listed by page number. History Nebraska photos and objects are credited only by their catalog or record group number.

1. RG3542-98-6
2. RG2065-1-11
3. 11055-1237
4. RG2499-1-1
5. RG1234-2-10
6. RG3064-26
7. RG802-60-1
8. History Nebraska Archeology
9. RG2183-1937-105-1
10. RG2063-50-2
11. RG2528-5-2x
12. RG2178-32
13. Sophia Smith Collection, Smith College Archives
14. 13053-72
15. RG1833-2-3
16. RG2158-24-7
17. Ben Kruse, History Nebraska
18. RG2608-1053
19. RG3542-141-4
20. RG2608-1063;
21. RG2608-2457a; RG2608-2537
22. RG3551-5
23. 9366-153; 2019 photo by History Nebraska
24. RG5899-11-3 (detail)
25. RG2339-595
26. RG825-3-1
27. RG2442-7-43
28. RG2442-7-4
29. RG2442-7-18
30. 11940-1-(1)
31. Top: RG5440-PH0; Bottom: Library of Congress Prints & Photographs
32. RG4290-715
33. RG3322-47
34. RG3097-8-1
35. RG2469-01
36. RG2113-3-2
37. RG2183-1930-1114-1
38. 1581-1
39. RG2411-3234
40. RG1085-24-7
41. RG3828-5-1
42. RG2183-1952-711-2
43. RG2418-3656
44. 1927
45. Courtesy of Colin and Brian Croft, Scottsbluff
46. RG2528-6-3
47. RG2158-37-34
48. RG2341-28
49. RG4290-535
50. RG2341-914
51. RG1234-19-4
52. RG2158-23
53. 13295-1
54-55. Gerald R. Ford Conservation Center, Omaha
56. RG2154-8-17
57. RG2536-5-133
58. RG3451-3-122
59. RG3384-7-2
60-61. New York Public Library
62. RG2451-50
63. RG3372-4-23
64. RG2341-343
65. 7619-66
66. RG3190-285x
67. RG1234-3-1
68. RG1714-15
69. RG1517-44-16
70. RG2186-5-108
71. RG2341-2
72. Courtesy of the Dawes County Historical Society, Chadron
73. 2012-186
74. 11055-2241-18
75. RG2963-11-22
76. RG2508-3
77. RG3882-310
78. RG3882-32b-368
79. RG3715-2-9
80. RG2772-1
81. RG3451-3-30
82. RG1073-4
83. RG2118-5-19
84. RG3348-10-11
85. RG2102-1-5
86. RG3882-21-163 (detail)
87. RG1667-7-1
88. RG3372-3-42
89. RG3542-132-12
90. Willa Cather Foundation, RG1951-1119
91. RG2587-1-9
92. RG3198-41-10
93. RG3361-11

94. RG3384-10-93
95. Painting by Titian Ramsay Peale,
    American Philosophical Society, Philadelphia;
    photo by History Nebraska
96. RG3882-17
97. RG2929-3-P
98. RG4062-3
99. RG5730-108
100. RG2758-104-10
101. RG856-9-57
102. RG2442
103. (Top) RG3319-1-45; (Bottom) RG3319-1-33
104. 11744-61
105. 2565-2
106. RG4290-399
107. RG1431-85-2
108. RG2348-4-1
109. 11088-1-(1-2)
110. Library of Congress Prints & Photographs
111. RG2521-0-25
112. RG2546-0-46
113. RG2499-5-1
114. 13338-39-1-13
115. RG14-x11
116-117. RG2341-58
118. 13361-1
119. RG4232-5-11
120. Badge: 7956-5986; detail of 1859 map,
    Colton's Kansas and Nebraska, M782 1859
    C72
121. 8631-2
122. RG2154-8-2
123. RG2669-5, RG2916.AM
124. RG3334-1-9
125. RG2491-2-123
126. Reprinted with permission from The Omaha
    World-Herald.
128. RG2018-71-11
129. RG3347-6-3
130. RG1576-2
131. RG2114-4-162
132. RG1289-25-36